INFORMATION
EXPLORER
JUNIOR

Being Respectful Online

by Ann Truesdell

CHERRY LAKE PUBLISHING · ANN ARBOR, MICHIGAN

CHERRY
LAKE
Publishing

Published in the United States of America
by Cherry Lake Publishing
Ann Arbor, Michigan
www.cherrylakepublishing.com

Content Adviser: Gail Dickinson, PhD, Associate Professor,
Old Dominion University, Norfolk, Virginia

Photo Credits: Cover, ©wong sze yuen/Shutterstock, Inc.; page 5, ©Dawn Shearer-
Simonetti/Shutterstock, Inc.; page 6, ©Twin Design/Shutterstock, Inc.; page 9,
©wavebreakmedia/Shutterstock, Inc.; page 10, © Lisa F. Young/Shutterstock,
Inc.; page 13, ©OtnaYdur/Shutterstock, Inc.; page 14, ©mmphotographie.de/
Shutterstock, Inc.; page 15, ©Catalin Petolea/Shutterstock, Inc.; page 17, ©Hung
Chung Chih/Shutterstock, Inc.; page 18, ©Mik Lav/Shutterstock, Inc.; page 20,
©Valua Vitaly/Shutterstock, Inc.

Library of Congress Cataloging-in-Publication Data
Truesdell, Ann.
  Being respectful online / by Ann Truesdell.
      pages cm. — (Information explorer junior)
  Includes bibliographical references and index.
  Audience: K to Grade 3.
  ISBN 978-1-62431-131-4 (lib. bdg.) — ISBN 978-1-62431-197-0 (e-book) —
ISBN 978-1-62431-263-2 (pbk.)
1. Online etiquette—Juvenile literature. 2. Internet—Moral and ethical aspects—
Juvenile literature. 3. Internet and children—Juvenile literature. I. Title.
  TK5105.878.T78 2014
  004.67'80835—dc23   2013012343

Cherry Lake Publishing would like to acknowledge the work of The Partnership for
21st Century Skills. Please visit *www.p21.org* for more information.

Printed in the United States of America
Corporate Graphics Inc.
July 2013
CLFA13

Table of Contents

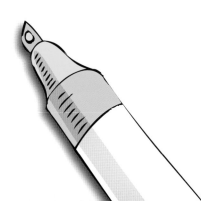

CHAPTER ONE

What Is a Cyberbully?

It can be fun to play games online.

It is fun to be online. The Internet lets you play with other kids without leaving your house! You can send messages to friends online. You can also play games together. It is important to remember that your online

Bullying can make kids feel sad or embarrassed.

friends are real people. You use good manners when you are playing with your friends in person. You should also be respectful online. Being respectful means treating others as you would want to be treated.

Being disrespectful online can hurt others' feelings. There is a special name for kids who pick on other people over the Internet. These kids are called **cyberbullies**. Cyberbullies are kids who are unkind to others online. They act the same as bullies do in person. They sometimes call others names or say mean things. They send hurtful e-mails or text messages. Other forms of cyberbullying include lying about people and telling secrets about others. Some cyberbullies even pretend to be someone else so they can make that person look bad. Bullying can hurt other people. There are things that you can do to help solve this problem. Read on to find out how!

Not all bullying happens in person.

To get a copy of this activity, visit www.cherrylakepublishing.com/activities.

Try This

How would you feel if someone said something mean to you in person? How would you feel if you got a mean e-mail? How are your feelings about the two situations alike or different? Do you think cyberbullying hurts more or less than bullying in person?

CHAPTER TWO

Don't Be a Bully

We follow rules that tell us how to be polite in public. This is called etiquette. There are also rules you should follow online. We call these rules **netiquette**. Following some simple netiquette rules can keep you from becoming a cyberbully.

Some rules of netiquette are easy to remember. They are a lot like etiquette. Did you know that TYPING IN ALL CAPITALS is considered yelling online? Yelling in public is considered rude. So is typing messages in all capital letters. Using another person's username is also bad netiquette. Logging in to someone else's accounts online is like going through his or her backpack. You shouldn't go through another person's belongings at school. You shouldn't do it online either. Spreading rumors and saying mean things are also wrong. Anything that hurts others in person will also hurt them in cyberspace.

If you type in all capitals, people online might think you are angry.

Most online communication is through some form of writing. This includes e-mails and instant messages. Some kids cyberbully by accident. They are not careful when they send written messages to others. Your friends can see your face when you talk to them. They know when you are joking because you might smile or make a silly face. But your words

A smile can let people know when you are joking.

stand alone when you write a message. Your friends cannot see your face. It is important to reread what you write before you send a message. Make sure that everything is spelled correctly. Proofread to make sure that your message says what you mean to say. Do you think someone could take your message the wrong way? Rewrite it or use **emoticons** to show what face you would make if you were talking in person.

Try This

Kelly wrote an e-mail to her friend Jenny. She reread her message before sending it. Some of her message needed rewording. Read the two e-mails below. How might Jenny understand the first e-mail? What parts of the e-mail might she find insulting? How is Kelly's reworded e-mail different than the first one? What important changes do you notice?

Hi Jenny,
Remember how I let you wear my shirt for your party last week? NOW YOU NEED TO BRING ME BACK THE SHIRT! Wash it first so that it's not stinky from you. I need to wear it to my piano recital.
~Kelly

Hi Jenny,
Can you please bring me back the shirt that I let you borrow for your party last week? I need to wear it for my piano recital on Tuesday. It would be great if you could wash it for me, too! :-) Thanks!
~Kelly

CHAPTER THREE

Respect Yourself

Consider your words carefully before posting online.

You should always respect others online. You also need to respect yourself!

Always think before you post anything online. Deleting a message or closing a window doesn't erase your words forever. Anything posted on the Internet can be recovered. This includes e-mails and messages you send to others. It also includes pictures and videos that you post. Is your post or message something that you would share without being embarrassed? Would you want everyone you know to see it? If not, you should avoid putting it online.

Would you feel embarrassed if someone saw your posts?

Talking to your parents can help you avoid problems online.

Do not share too much personal information online. This includes the information you share with friends. Keep your passwords private. They should be shared only with your parents. Your parents can help guide you online. They are responsible for you. Help them by keeping them informed. Tell them what you are doing online. Listen to their suggestions. They can help keep you safe.

To get a copy of this activity, visit www.cherrylakepublishing.com/activities.

Try This

How much information about yourself can you find online? Type your name into a search engine. See what comes up. Is your home address or phone number online? Can you find pictures or videos of yourself? Show an adult what you find. Does anyone besides your parents or teachers know your passwords? Change them. Make sure not to share the new ones with other people.

CHAPTER FOUR

If It Happens to You

What would you do if someone sent you a hurtful message?

You do your best to be respectful online to yourself and others. But you might still receive a mean picture or video or a rude comment on a Web site. What should you do if you get a mean message?

Don't be afraid to show an adult the evidence if you are cyberbullied.

Don't respond to the cyberbully's message. They want you to respond so they can send you messages back. The bully might get bored and stop if you do not reply. Kids sometimes reply to hurtful messages because they are angry. Your reply might be mean if you send a message when you are angry. Then you become a cyberbully yourself. It's best to not respond at all.

Save any messages you get from cyberbullies. You may want to delete a mean message and forget about the whole thing. It is better to save the message as proof of the bullying.

Show the message to your parents or another trusted adult, such as a teacher. An adult can help you come up with a plan to stop the bullying. The principal or counselors at your school may even help you with the situation. Cyberbullying has happened to many kids. School administrators are often very good at coming up with plans to work things out.

Don't delete a mean message. You may need it for proof of the bullying.

Talk to an adult about your feelings. It's normal to feel sad or angry when you are cyberbullied. An adult can help you sort through your feelings. Talking to someone can also make you feel better. Cyberbullying is a big problem for many people. Take the right steps to prevent it from happening to you or others. Then you can safely enjoy all of the great things the Internet has to offer!

Don't let cyberbullies ruin the Internet for you!

To get a copy of this activity, visit www.cherrylakepublishing.com/activities.

Try This

Talk to classmates and trusted adults about bullying. Share your experiences. Then ask the others to share their own experiences with bullying. Have you ever witnessed someone being bullied? Have you ever been bullied yourself? How did you feel? What did you learn from that experience? How does it change the way that you treat others? What can you do to stop cyberbullying at your school?

Make a poster to hang at school.

21

Glossary

cyberbullies **(SY-bur-bul-eez)** people who use technology to pick on others

emoticons **(i-MOH-ti-kahnz)** small images of faces expressing different emotions, used in e-mail or instant messaging to communicate feelings or attitudes

netiquette **(NET-i-kit)** rules or guidelines for good online behavior

Find Out More

BOOKS

Criswell, Patti Kelley. *Stand Up for Yourself and Your Friends: Dealing with Bullies and Bossiness and Finding a Better Way*. Middleton, WI: American Girl, 2009.

Ludwig, Trudy. *Confessions of a Former Bully*. Berkeley, CA: Tricycle Press, 2010.

Polacco, Patricia. *Bully*. New York: G. P. Putnam's Sons, 2012.

WEB SITES

StopBullying.gov

www.stopbullying.gov

This U.S. government Web site provides tips for preventing bullying and informs kids how to respond when they are bullied.

STOP Cyberbullying

www.stopcyberbullying.org

Find out what you can do to help end cyberbullying in your community.

Index

About the Author

Ann Truesdell is a school library media specialist and teacher in Michigan. She and her husband, Mike, are the proud parents of James, Charlotte, and Matilda. She enjoys traveling and reading.